MANHATTAN

A Photographic Journey

TEXT: **Bill Harris**

CAPTIONS: **Pauline Graham**

DESIGNED BY: **Teddy Hartshorn**

PICTURE EDITOR: **Annette Lerner**

PHOTOGRAPHY: **CLB and Karen Kent**

EDITORIAL: **Pauline Graham**

PRODUCTION: **Ruth Arthur and David Proffit**

DIRECTOR OF PRODUCTION: **Gerald Hughes**

CLB 2706
© 1990 Colour Library Books Ltd., Godalming, Surrey, England.
All rights reserved.
This 1993 edition is published by Crescent Books,
distributed by Outlet Book Company, Inc., a Random House Company,
40 Engelhard Avenue, Avenel, New Jersey 07001.

Random House
New York • Toronto • London • Sydney • Auckland

Printed and bound in Singapore

ISBN 0-517-07388-9

8 7 6 5 4 3 2 1

MANHATTAN

A Photographic Journey

Text by
BILL HARRIS

CRESCENT BOOKS
NEW YORK • AVENEL, NEW JERSEY

At the edge of Columbia University's Baker Field, on the northern tip of Manhattan Island, there is a big rock where the path winds off into the woods. It holds a plaque proclaiming that this is the very spot where Peter Minuit bought the island from the Indians for sixty guilders in 1626.

No one disputes the tradition that sixty 17th-century Dutch guilders translates into twenty-four 20th-century American dollars, but the rock may be in the wrong place. The people of Holland have erected a flagpole in Battery Park, 13 miles away at the southern tip of Manhattan Island, with an inscription that says it happened down there.

Who's right? Who knows?

The Dutch kept careful records, but they weren't too strong on keeping track of specific spots where great events took place. It was probably because they were so busy moving the spots around. From the earliest times they were digging canals, leveling hills, filling in low places and extending the shoreline. Hardly a day has gone by since they first came here that Manhattan hasn't changed in some way.

It's what makes the place so exciting.

In fact, if old Peter Minuit were to come back to Manhattan today, the only place he'd probably recognize is Inwood Hill Park, a 196-acre virgin wilderness a block or two away from that rock whose plaque says he once stood nearby with his bag of beads and trinkets. He might be a little surprised by the Henry Hudson Parkway that cuts through the middle of it, or the 142-foot-high Henry Hudson Bridge, a steel arch that carries cars into The Bronx. But he'd still find the caves Indians used for shelter and the steep hills that once characterized much of Manhattan. He'd also recognize the little bay in the Harlem River which is said to have been the first place Henry Hudson went ashore when he arrived in 1609. But even recent Columbia alumnae who haven't been back to a football game at Baker Field, which overlooks the bay, wouldn't recognize the old stadium. It's been modernized, rebuilt, changed.

Of all the change in upper Manhattan, the strangest may well be the one that has relocated a piece of the borough to The Bronx.

In Colonial times, the northern boundary of Manhattan was a winding creek that connected the Harlem River on the east with the Hudson River on the west. The Dutch called it *Spuyten Duyvil* because, according to Washington Irving's Father Knickerbocker, an early settler named Anthony Van Corlaer drowned there on his way to warn the northern settlements that the British were coming. The Dutch, says Knickerbocker, thought the Devil lived in the deep, wild waters of the creek. Van Corlaer couldn't find a boat to get him across, but he'd had enough rum to make an easy decision to swim across in spite of the Devil, or as he said in Dutch, "en spijt den Duyvil."

The Devil was evicted and the creek rerouted in 1895 when a 400- foot-wide ship channel was cut through to connect the Harlem and Hudson Rivers. In the process a 52-acre knob of territory that had formerly been a part of Manhattan Island became, geographically at least, a piece of The Bronx. But New Yorkers are funny about things like that. They got up a petition and convinced City Hall that their neighborhood, called Marble Hill because of the quarries there, still had its heart in Manhattan. The city fathers took their plea to heart, and though some people who live there may tell you they live in the Kingsbridge section of The Bronx, they're as much Manhattanites as if they lived in Greenwich Village.

And they're not alone in their isolation from the main island. Halfway down the East River, where the 59th Street Bridge crosses over into Queens, some 6,000 people who get to Manhattan in an overhead cable car from

Roosevelt Island qualify as Manhattanites, too. They try to keep non-residents out by not selling the required subway tokens at the Second Avenue Tramway station, but many of their neighbors from the west side of the river, using a little foresight, take the trip anyway. Roosevelt Island is a nice place for a picnic, but there's a better reason for going. The view of Manhattan from there is glorious, which is more than can be said of the view of the two-and-a-half-mile island from the other side.

In the early 1970s, city planners decided to cover the island with a series of apartment communities. Mercifully, only one, a complex of some 2,000 apartments, was actually built. The cheaper apartments overlook Queens and, ironically, the most expensive are at the northern end of the town, the longest walk from the tram. Walking is necessary because cars are banned from Roosevelt Island. It can be reached by car from Queens, but the road leads directly to a parking garage and goes no further.

If the new buildings on Roosevelt Island are banal, there are some gems the developers never got around to destroying and a couple they've even restored. The 18th-century Blackwell farmhouse is among them, as is the Chapel of the Good Shepherd, built in 1889. But the most interesting is a lighthouse at the northern tip that legend says was built by an inmate of an insane asylum that once stood nearby. According to the story, John McCarthy came from Ireland with an unnatural fixation, even for an Irishman, that the British were after him. When he was finally institutionalized, the warden saw nothing wrong with allowing him to build a fort at the end of the island to defend them all against a British attack. When the city decided to build a lighthouse on the spot, they had to deal with old John who finally agreed to tear down his fort if they would let him build the lighthouse. He may have been a certified lunatic, but he did a good job. On the other hand, he had good plans to work from. The 50-foot granite tower was designed by James Renwick, the architect of Saint Patrick's Cathedral. Renwick also designed the buildings at the south end of the island which are now boarded up and falling apart. When they were new, they were used as a hospital for smallpox victims.

Roosevelt Island was once called Blackwell's Island for the family who owned it. In 1921 its name was changed to Welfare Island because of the city hospitals and the lunatic asylum that were there. Though there are two city hospitals still operating on the island, it somehow didn't seem right to have high-rent apartments in a place with a name like that and so, in 1973, it got a more genteel name.

Further up the river, Ward's Island and Randall's Island, connected by landfill, are also technically a part of Manhattan. Except for patients in the hospitals there, no one lives on either island, but their parks, reached from Manhattan by a footbridge at 103d Street, are a beautiful escape from the streets of the city on a hot summer afternoon.

Randall's Island is also headquarters of the Triborough Bridge and Tunnel Authority and is the point where the bridge itself splits in three different directions to serve The Bronx, Queens and Manhattan.

But except for those outposts, Manhattan is a tidy little self-contained island 13 miles long and less than three miles wide. Though it is the smallest of New York City's five boroughs, it's home to about a million-and-a-half people and host to more than 17 million tourists each year, not to mention more than 4 million people who commute there each day to work. At any given moment on a busy day, as many people as the populations of Alaska, Montana, Maine and Minnesota *combined* may be just visiting and sharing Manhattan's 22.6 square miles with the people who live there. Many of the visitors stay a while, an average of four days, and there are 100,000 hotel rooms to accommodate them. Paris and Rome together have about 88,000 hotel rooms, but Paris and Rome together don't add up to one Manhattan.

Manhattan, for instance, has more marble in churches, building lobbies and facades than all of Rome, and it has as many French restaurants as Paris. Better still, it has 49 other distinct cuisines to choose from. It has more museums and art galleries, over 500 of them, than London; and more skyscrapers than any city in the world. At last count the number was edging close to a thousand, but the builders are working hard to improve on that.

The builders never stop, in fact. If you haven't been to Manhattan in a month, there are things you won't recognize. But almost nothing they do compares with the building project that began in the center of town when they started digging a hole on Fifth Avenue between 49th and 50th Streets in July, 1931.

When the plans for developing the area were shown to the public that spring, *The New York Times* had called it a collection of "architectural aberrations and monstrosities." But *The Times* isn't *always* right. The buildings that would be called Rockefeller Center are possibly the best thing that has happened to New York in the 20th century.

But it wasn't what anyone had in mind at the beginning. The story really begins in 1926 when the trustees of the Metropolitan Opera Company decided that their opera house, the focal point of New York's social world, was not only outdated but in a bad neighborhood. It was located on Broadway at 39th Street, a section that was beginning at that time to become the heart of the city's garment industry. The idea of dodging push carts in their fancy cars offended a lot of opera-goers and a committee was formed to find a better location.

Several sites were considered, but the best turned out to be a large parcel of land owned by Columbia University on Fifth Avenue between 48th and 51st Streets. It was a good location and getting better in spite of the fact it was in the middle of the city's speak-easy district and many of the buildings around it were down at the heels. The Opera Company began making plans. Their architect, Benjamin Wistar Morris, proposed a complex of buildings that included placing the Opera House in the middle of the block between Fifth and Sixth Avenues. He would create a new north-south street in front of it and a great plaza surrounded by revenue-producing shops and restaurants. The rest of the site would be used for office buildings that would also bring income to the Opera Company. His plan was greeted with warm praise, but nobody thought it was such a good idea to give so much valuable real estate over to an open plaza that would never produce a dime of income.

Money was already a problem. Among the people who were asked to contribute generously was John D. Rockefeller, Jr., who agreed to finance the land acquisition. He had a lease negotiated and then offered to sell it to the Opera Company at cost through a long-term mortgage which he himself would finance. The proposal was made in the summer of 1929. In the fall of 1929, the stock market collapsed and along with it so did the Metropolitan Opera's enthusiasm for moving to a better neighborhood. Rockefeller was left with a long-term lease on land whose value was falling as the Great Depression increased.

Rockefeller later wrote that he had two choices: to abandon the project entirely or to make something of it. "...To go forward with it in the definite knowledge that I would have to build and finance it alone, without the immense impetus that the new opera house would have given, and with no escape from the fact that under the changed conditions it would be necessary to improve all the land in order to lease it, thus involving immense capital outlays never contemplated."

Rockefeller had long-since drawn up plans for the area around the Opera House, but without it his plans needed to be much more grandiose. He assembled a group of architects, including Raymond Hood and Wallace K. Harrison, who worked and reworked a variety of plans, all of which retained Benjamin Morris's scheme for an open plaza, a promenade and shopping arcades. But where Morris had contemplated a 12-story building surrounded by office towers at the edges of the site, their plan, evolved over four years of work, called for a dramatic office tower on the opera house site with lower buildings complementing it in the three surrounding blocks.

A dramatic office tower needs a dramatic tenant and the one that made the whole thing work was Radio Corporation of America. RCA was growing by leaps and bounds in the late 1920s and even the most disinterested observer would agree its future was even brighter. The company had built its own corporate headquarters at the corner of Lexington Avenue and 51st Street in 1927, but was outgrowing the space. Through a complex set of financial dealings, they turned the building over to the General Electric Corporation in settlement of a debt and began looking around for something more suitable. Rockefeller had their answer.

Negotiations were finished in early 1930 and Rockefeller's office complex had not only a major tenant but a whole point of view. An internal memo discussing the possibilities told him, "...Due to inventions like the Victrola and the radio, the costs of opera can now be spread over wide geographical areas and the best singers and artists can be retained at salaries which a single opera company can no longer afford to pay...(We are) thinking of a pretty large combination which would include a Carnegie Hall, an Opera House, a theater, business offices." The original plan had come full circle and culture was brought back into the picture. In its contract, which called for an entertainment complex that would include two theaters, two office buildings and a broadcast center for the exclusive use of the National Broadcasting Company, RCA was given the right to give it a name. It was a brilliant choice: *Radio City*.

There ought to be a prettier word to describe the architectural style of the 70-story RCA Building, but the plan is known in the trade as a "slab." It's one of the earliest examples of a slab building and still one of the best. Credit for that goes to Raymond Hood, the architect, who modified a simple rectangular box with dramatic setbacks that make it look like a building on the move, a perfect image for a company like RCA. In the early planning stages a Rockefeller executive had told him, "I have never collected an extra dollar of rent for space more than 30 feet from a window." When the building was finished, Hood couldn't help bragging that "there is not a single point in the rentable area of the building that is more than 22 feet away from a window." Not only that, it had the largest floor area of any commercial building in the world at the time.

At the same time the RCA tower was going up, work was going forward on the 31-story RKO Building, the Center Theater (converted in 1954 to an office building) and Radio City Music Hall.

The Music Hall is the biggest indoor theater in the world, but it's much more than that. It's arguably the most beautiful. All of Rockefeller Center is adorned with murals, sculpture and architectural details that are among the best in the world. But the interior designer of the Music Hall, Donald Deskey, warned the architects before they hired him that he wouldn't be a slave to the "dry, formal academic treatment of the past" as, in his opinion, they had been. He promised them a contemporary effect and that's what he gave them. A walk through the Music Hall today is like taking a trip back in time to 1932, and what a pleasure it is.

The man who breathed life into Radio City Music Hall was Samuel Rothafel, a showman who called himself "Roxy." He once summed up his philosophy when he said, "We don't produce the pictures. Some are good and some are not so good. But we can build the show around the picture on the theory that if the appetizer is good and the dessert is good, the entree will be acceptable even if only fair." His career seemed to have reached its apex in 1927 when he opened a 6,000-seat theater at 50th Street and Seventh Avenue which he modestly named "The Roxy." It was a baroque masterpiece, the most expensive theater ever built. But in 1930, he moved down the block to Radio City. He was chasing a dream. "I didn't conceive the idea," he said. "I dreamt it, I believe in creative dreams."

His dream turned out to be a nightmare for his new bosses. Roxy's idea was to use the Music Hall as a vaudeville house. He had pioneered the idea of presenting stage shows along with movies, but he explained, "I thought it would embellish and bring out the movies. Now I think the presentation has outgrown its usefulness. The motion pictures have gone away from this. They speak for themselves. They no longer need such aid. They have grown up. Now I am going to do something else. No movies will be shown at Radio City Music Hall."

His opening night, on December 27, 1932, was a spectacular that lasted more than six hours and offended every critic in town. Patrons stayed away in record numbers, overcoming even their natural curiosity to see the new theater, and it lost an average of $90,000 a week. Meanwhile, Roxy had opened another theater in the new Rockefeller Center complex at the corner of 49th Street and Sixth Avenue. In spite of the fact that it was two short blocks from his Seventh Avenue namesake, he called it the RKO Roxy. At the new Roxy he did what he knew best, combining a film and stage show. It was a hit and less than a month after the Music Hall opened, the stage and screen show was moved to the larger theater. In 1932, a half-dozen New York theaters featured stage shows with first-run movies. Roxy was right, though, it was an idea that had outgrown its usefulness. But it lasted at Radio City Music Hall until 1979.

Roxy was only one of the reasons. There were two others and he hired both of them. One was the director of production, Leon Leonidoff, who took full advantage of the Hall's spectacular stage facilities to produce shows the like of which no one had ever seen before. The other was his associate, Russel Markert, who created the world's first precision dance team, called *The Rockets*, in St. Louis in the early '20s. Roxy hired them to be part of the show at his Roxy theater and renamed them *The Roxyettes*. They went along with him to the new Music Hall and long outlasted him there. When poor health and poor business forced him to resign in 1933, a PR genius at Rockefeller Center changed their name to *The Rockettes* and ever since, the name has been as synonymous with New York as the Statue of Liberty, the Empire State Building and even Rockefeller Center itself.

But if show business made Rockefeller Center exciting, the planners had other kinds of tenants in mind, too. One of John D. Rockefeller's major interests was the improvement of international relations and its corollary, international trade. Though New York is the most international of all cities today, its major connection with the great capitals of Europe in the early '30s was mostly in the faces of its immigrant citizens. Rockefeller proposed that the three blocks of Fifth Avenue frontage that were part of his new Center become a landmark to international friendship.

Two low buildings between 49th and 50th Streets were planned to dramatize the soaring RCA Building even more while at the same time serving as a gateway to the Center itself. The downtown structure was designated "Palais de France"; its neighbor to the north, the "British Empire Building." Each would contain retail shops and office space rented by the governments of the two countries. The space between, naturally, became known as the "Channel Gardens."

The enthusiasm among foreign governments for the idea led to the creation of plans for two similar buildings in the block uptown, across Fifth Avenue from Saint Patrick's Cathedral. The tenants were to be Italy and Germany. But war was on its way in Europe and though the Palazzo d'Italia eventually became a reality, the proposed Deutches Haus was renamed International Building North. The International Building itself, a 40-story structure fronted by Lee Lawrie's heroic sculpture of Atlas, was opened in 1933. Fifty years later, it still has possibly more different international tenants than any building of its size in Manhattan.

Lawrie's Atlas may be the second-most photographed piece of sculpture in Manhattan. The first (discounting the Statue of Liberty, of course, which, after all, isn't in Manhattan) has to be Paul Manship's Prometheus, which looks down on summer diners and winter skaters in the Center's sunken Plaza; that same plaza that was the most controversial part of Benjamin Morris's plan for developing the area around an opera house and became one of the few elements of it that remain.

Having a square-foot Plaza in a neighborhood where commercial rents are so high would make a corporate comptroller speechless. But hardly anybody ever visits Manhattan without a visit to Rockefeller Plaza and the feeling they take away with them is priceless. Even in Manhattan there are things money can't buy.

John D. Rockefeller and his sons gave Manhattan much more than their famous "city within a city." Rockefeller University, a six- block enclave along the East River running north from 62d Street, was established by John D. Rockefeller, Sr. in 1901 as a center for medical education and research. In the years since, 16 of its faculty have won Nobel Prizes for, among other things, the isolation of antibiotics, the first demonstration that DNA transmits hereditary factors, and finding a way to preserve whole blood, a discovery that made blood banks possible.

It was Rockefeller money and John D. Rockefeller, Jr's enthusiasm that made Riverside Church, overlooking the Hudson River at 121st Street, an uptown landmark that lures more visitors up Riverside Drive than nearby Grant's Tomb, which ranked as the city's number one tourist attraction in the last century.

But visitors have a better reason for going uptown, and Rockefeller made that possible, too. It's the Cloisters, a branch of the Metropolitan Museum of Art, high on a hill surrounded by parkland with a view of the Hudson River Palisades. The building, the parks, even the view, are all the result of Rockefeller philanthropies.

It began when George Grey Barnard, a sculptor and art collector, came home from France with an accumulation of medieval art treasures that he put on display. His little, private museum was bought intact about ten years later by the Metropolitan Museum of Art with money provided by Rockefeller, who also donated some other medieval objects from his own collection.

At the same time, he gave the city 66 acres of land in Northern Manhattan, which he had bought many years before and had landscaped as a park. The northern end of the park, named for Fort Tryon, George Washington's last outpost before retreating from Manhattan in November, 1776, was reserved as the setting for a museum that would be called The Cloisters.

Before beginning construction, Rockefeller bought a stretch of land across the river in New Jersey and gave it to the state for a park which would guarantee that the view from The Cloisters would never include a high-rise apartment house or suburban housing tract. Then he went to work to guarantee that the view from New Jersey would be terrific, too. The view would be of a medieval-*looking* building perched on a tree-covered hillside.

Many people think that the building is the genuine article and not just a medieval-looking building. But the fact is, it was brand-new in 1938. The inside does contain chapels and cloisters and architectural elements that date back as far as the 12th century, brought to Manhattan from Europe and reconstructed. But the granite in the building's exterior was quarried in Connecticut and the Belgian blocks that are used for paving were dug up from Manhattan streets.

While John D. Rockefeller, Jr. was creating a home for medieval art in Manhattan, his wife, Abby Aldrich Rockefeller, was busy with an entirely different kind of building and an entirely different kind of art. Along with Lillie P. Bliss and Mrs. Cornelius J. Sullivan, Mrs. Rockefeller's interest ranged toward modern art, and within a year of the opening of The Cloisters, Edward Durrell Stone and Phillip L. Goodwin's tile and glass Museum of Modern Art elbowed out the row of early brownstones and townhouses that had made West 53rd Street a pleasant place to live, and opened America's eyes to the work of such artists as Picasso, Matisse, Van Gogh and Mondrian.

Though the earliest works in the collection date back to the late 19th century, the Museum has kept pace and more than a third of its collection is work produced since the end of World War II. And a recent renovation that includes a 50-story apartment tower has more than doubled the space to display it in.

No matter what interests anyone, there is probably a museum that heightens that interest somewhere in Manhattan. Con Edison, the power company, has an Energy Museum at its headquarters on 14th Street; the Fire Department has three floors of colorful apparatus in an old Duane Street firehouse, and the biggest collection of memorabilia related to law and order in the United States is at the Police Academy Museum on East 20th Street. There is a museum on West 83rd Street designed for participation by children, and on East 53rd, people who were children when Howdy Doody kept them quiet can relive the experience at the Museum of Broadcasting. Subjects from advertising to coin-collecting, Bible study to the American theater all have their own special place in Manhattan. But possibly the most unusual is also the newest, even though it's in one of Manhattan's oldest sections. It's called South Street Seaport.

The neighborhood around the corner of Fulton and Water Streets was the heart of the Port of New York in the 18th and 19th centuries. In the summer of 1983 part of it was restored, part of it recreated, as a waterfront historic district. The developers claim that the eleven-block area is a preservation of the spirit of the old neighborhood with a contemporary experience added. It's a charming place, but not because it accurately recaptures the spirit of the past. One hundred years ago, it was a neighborhood best avoided. Consider this contemporary account, written in 1874:

"The neighborhood of Water Street...abounds in lodging-houses for sailors, liquor stores of the lowest class without number, dance houses and concert saloons and various other low places of amusement. Brothels of the worst description swarm in all directions...The infamous proprietors of dance and sailors' lodging-houses seem to consider that a staff of prostitutes is a necessary part of their stock in trade; a stock, if anything, more remunerative than the sale of their villainous whisky.

"At night the quarrels, fights and noisy disturbances make the darkness hideous, and are of such frequency that none can hope for a night's rest...Fights and desperate encounters among intoxicated men and women occur night after night and are looked upon as a regular part of the twenty-four hours' program...The use of deadly weapons, too, is so common that murder provokes no sentiment of horror among the denizens of Water Street, but only excites in them a morbid curiosity to see the murderer as he is hauled off to jail by the police.

"And if they have homes, what are they? The men, too often confirmed drunkards, and consequently continually out of work and unable to support their families honestly; the women — oh, horrible thought! — earning the wages of sin with the consent of their husbands; the children literally brought up in the gutter; clothes, furniture, bedding, all gone to the pawnshop; the whole family huddled together at night on a dirty husk or straw mattress, or on the bare boards in one ill-built, badly- ventilated and filthy room where any pretense at decency is impossible."

Exactly 110 years later, the following classified ad appeared in *The New York Times*:

South Street Seaport
$2100
1BR luxury apt. Elev. building.
24hr. Concierge, 12' ceilings,
large picture windows overlooking
turn of century street.

And that may well be a bargain, even though the nearest supermarket may be ten blocks away and there is no laundromat or dry cleaner within walking distance. If it's within walking distance of the Seaport, even though the picture windows obviously don't overlook the River, it's worth more than a meager $2,100 a month.

As recently as ten years ago, you probably could have rented a retail store in the neighborhood for less. Everyone knew the restoration was coming; historic ships were tied up to Pier 16 on the East River at Fulton Street and volunteers were working hard to restore them. New, nondescript stainless steel and glass office towers were blossoming on Water Street, but somehow no one really believed that the restored Seaport would ever be much more than an opportunity for people who enjoy such things as chipping rust, sanding wood and repairing beautiful, old sailing ships.

But then one day it all came together. Two blocks of fine old buildings were restored and space in them rented for restaurants, antique stores, craft shops. Galleries were added, a special multi-media theater was created. Across the street from the Museum, residents of a nursing home were shuffled off to another part of town and the building renovated for luxury cooperative apartments. Construction was quickly finished on a 35-story hulk of an office building that effectively walls off the Seaport and separates the 19th century from the 20th. It was built in such a hurry, in fact, that the remains of an old sailing ship were unexpectedly uncovered during excavation for the foundation, but were hurriedly covered up again so as not to interrupt the tight building schedule.

The block of Fulton Street from Water Street to the River has been repaved with cobblestones to give it a more authentic 19th- century look. In those days, the streets of most coastal cities, including New York, were paved with the stones which sometimes go by the more up-scale name of

Belgian blocks. The huge sailing ships that took furs, rum and tobacco and other such necessities to Europe often came back comparatively empty and the squared stones were loaded aboard as ballast to keep them from tipping over. Most were dumped into the harbor and used as landfill but some survived as paving material. Mercifully, the cobblestoned block of Fulton Street is closed to traffic. They're no fun at all to drive on.

That same block is the only one in Manhattan were it's legal to drink on the street, except in sidewalk cafes, and on nice summer evenings young Wall Street types stroll up and down with very British-looking pints of ale from the North Star Pub. The Pub is new, but it's in a carefully-restored row of buildings built by speculator Peter Schermerhorn in 1811. Though it once contained the kind of establishment that made "decent" folks avoid the neighborhood, it's quite respectable these days. It contains a gift shop run by the Seaport Museum, a branch of the famous Strand Bookstore and a selection of shops that sell all sorts of things from Irish sweaters to sou'westers to running shoes.

One tenant of the restored building is a second-floor restaurant called *Sweets*, which has been serving seafood there since 1842, making it the oldest such establishment in the city. When the building was redone, so was *Sweets* and as often happens it got more cuteness than character, but they were smart enough to go back to the original. They never did change the original quality of the food, apparently on the theory that "if it ain't broke, don't fix it." Nor did they change their hours. Even though the Seaport is a bustling place well into the evening, no one gets into *Sweets* after 8:30.

Another South Street old-timer is just around the corner in the same row, though it's a comparative newcomer. The restaurant called *Sloppy Louie's* has been there since the mid-1930s, which, come to think of it, is a ripe old age for a Manhattan restaurant.

Though it looks old, the Fulton Market building across Fulton Street from the Schermerhorn Row was finished in 1983, replacing an extension of the Fulton Fish Market that was established in 1822. It's a three-story building crammed with shops that sell everything from clam chowder to cashews. There are restaurants offering nouvelle cuisine and fresh seafood, an ice cream shop that sells "sorbets and gelatti," and a macaroni shop that dispenses "pasta." (Very turn of the century!) You can buy a dill pickle from a barrel there, or a bouquet of flowers. You can pick up a loaf of bread and just about any kind of cheese you ever heard of. You can watch the whole scene from a piano bar or a sushi bar. You can even, believe it or not, buy fresh fish there.

The block of buildings at Fulton and Water Streets more accurately reflect the past, even though the names of some of the shops run toward today's East Side-quaint. A toy store is called *Gepetto's*, specially designed accessories are available at *Laughing Stock* and you can get handpainted clothing at *Foofaraw*. But it's the row that contains the Museum's Gallery, a store that specializes in charts and nautical books, a shop that prints cards and stationery the old-fashioned way and the very up-to- the-minute Seaport Theater. It presents a slide and film show every hour that gives a quick, but thorough, history of New York as a major seaport. It's more than just a visual experience. One point in the show, describing the trip in a clipper ship from New York to San Francisco around the tip of South America, is literally guaranteed to give you goosebumps.

South Street was New York's major waterfront from the earliest days because the East River never freezes over in the winter months. After the Civil War, when iron-clad ships were beginning to use the port, ice was not a worry any longer and shipping moved to the deeper North River piers on the West Side. The Fulton Ferry to Brooklyn kept the neighborhood active until it was replaced by the Brooklyn Bridge and then life began passing it by.

In the mid-1960s, volunteers began work on restoring the area around piers 15 and 16. In time, they acquired and refurbished an 1885 English square-rigger called *The Wavertree* and a four-masted bark, *The Peking*, built in Germany in 1811. Their fleet was complemented with the 1893 Gloucester schooner, *Lettie G. Howard*, a 1912 steam lighter, *New York Central No. 29* and a 1925 steam ferryboat, *Major General William H. Hart*. Possibly the most historic ship in the collection is the *Ambrose*, a lightship that marked the entrance to New York harbor through a ship channel designed in 1899 by John Wolfe Ambrose. The lightship was anchored out there in 1907 and never went anywhere until 1932 when she was replaced and towed back into the harbor.

But if history is a secondary concern, one of the Museum's ships, the schooner *Pioneer*, built in 1885, is still a working vessel. What she works at is pleasure. Except in the dead of winter, she cruises the harbor giving visitors a taste of what all water travel was like in the days before 1807 when Robert Fulton sailed up the Hudson in a steam-powered boat he called the *Clermont*.

Fulton's journey took him, in a shower of sparks, all the way to Albany and back. It began at a pier at the end of West 10th Street in the heart of Greenwich Village.

In a city where change is such an important fact of life, a part of Manhattan that looks more like the 19th century than any other, including the South Street area, is the section bounded by the Hudson River, Houston Street, Broadway and 14th Street, the district of winding streets and old houses called Greenwich Village.

But appearances can be deceiving. The Village, like the rest of Manhattan, has gone through several incarnations and though the Landmarks Preservation Commission works hard at keeping up appearances, there are no anarchists making bombs in the basements and the writers and poets who live there are much more well-heeled than the ones who made it the world capital of Bohemianism back in the 1920s.

The shock that Bohemianism had deserted Greenwich Village in the face of high post-war rents hit hard in the 1960s when young people began migrating to the big cities in search of freedom to wear long hair and dirty dungarees and to protest the mess their parents had presumably gotten the world into. In New York, the natural gathering point for such people was by tradition Greenwich Village. But the people who were already there, probably the most tolerant of any community in the world, didn't want them as neighbors, though they didn't mind letting them hang out in the streets or in Washington Square Park. Their weapon was high rents. The hippies, as they called themselves, found a more favorable climate east of Third Avenue and when they moved in, they thumbed their nose at the establishment by calling their adopted neighborhood the "East Village." Old established Village people still cringe when they hear their neighborhood called the "West Village," but that's only one way things have changed.

It was an Indian village in the beginning and then a Dutch tobacco plantation. When the English took over it became the country estate of Sir Peter Warren, a Vice Admiral of the British Fleet. His widow inherited the place and her family, the De Lanceys, divided it up into building lots.

Among the estates established in this quiet little suburban town was Richmond Hill, located where Charlton and Varick Streets meet today. George Washington lived there in the summer of 1776. When he became

President in New York, he moved to a house on the now-vanished Cherry Street, not far from the Water Street seaport district. But his Vice President, John Adams, moved uptown to the Richmond Hill estate, which became the home of Aaron Burr after the Capital was moved.

Though it had become a mecca for all the important people in Colonial New York, the Village kept its rural character. Even the establishment of a State Prison on West 10th Street in 1797 didn't change things much, though it did bring new people into the neighborhood. That same year, a yellow fever epidemic brought them in hordes. It was believed that the best way to escape the disease was to get to high ground and the highest ground nearest the city was Greenwich Village, which in that year became New York City's most important suburb, the only one with scheduled stagecoach service between it and the city.

In 1811, when the City Commissioners decreed that all of Manhattan's streets should be laid out in a gridiron pattern and should be numbered, it was far too late to do anything about the tangle of streets in the Village, some of which followed the routes of old Indian trails or the boundaries of farms which had often been established by such things as the location of a certain tree. But the plan did have some effect on the Village when it called for a formal square to be placed on the site of Potter's Field, and a broad avenue running north from the center of it that would be called "Fifth." The square itself would be called the "Washington Military Parade Ground."

It took them until 1819 to stop holding public hangings in the square and to move Potter's Field further uptown. In 1828, when the first stretch of Fifth Avenue extended all the way up to 13th Street, people began taking it seriously as a residential neighborhood. Within five years, a fine row of houses walled in the north side of the square, making it the most prestigious pair of blocks in all of Manhattan with all the "old money" represented there by names like Roosevelt and Brevoort, Hamilton, Whetmore and Phelpse. Later in the century, when such nouveau riche families as the Vanderbilts and Astors began establishing themselves further uptown, the Washington Square North crowd stayed put and in the process preserved the houses and the neighborhood, which aren't much changed even today.

All through the second half of the 19th century, Greenwich Village north of the Square and east of the Sixth Avenue Elevated Railroad was home to all the best people including merchant princes, war heroes and, of course, the old established families who were known as the "Knickerbockers."

The eastern side of the square was established as the campus of New York University in the mid-1830s and the blocks to the east of it were small factories, sweatshops and office buildings. South of the Square was territory reserved for immigrant families and the working poor. East of Sixth Avenue was home to the middle class, the tracks of the Sixth Avenue El making a fine, natural dividing line.

Though Greenwich Village's 19th-century history is easily traced through its houses, there is only one building in all of the Village that dates back to the 18th century, even though it has been a settled area since 1668. It's a recently-restored farmhouse on the corner of Commerce and Bedford Streets that just squeaks by, having been built in 1798.

For all its historic charm, it's the legends of the 20th century that visitors flock there for, but possibly not one of them would have been established if the charm had not been there in the first place.

Artists and writers had begun finding low rents on the south side of Washington Square right after the turn of the century, but the place became a Mecca for them in December, 1912 when a woman named Mabel Dodge came to New York and took up residence at 23 Fifth Avenue at the corner of Ninth Street.

She had lived in Paris for ten years where she said she had discovered what it was like "to be alive like fire." Among the people who kept the fire going for her there were Pablo Picasso, the actor Gordon Craig and Gertrude Stein. Her sojourn came to an end when it was time to send her son to school and she rejected the idea of having him educated in Paris. She didn't particularly like New York, but settled on the one neighborhood in the city that reminded her of her adopted city in France.

That same year, 1912, America seemed to have suddenly turned intellectual. They were buying books of poetry by Vachel Lindsay and Amy Lowell and even avidly followed the controversy over whether a New England teenager named Edna St. Vincent Millay had been unfairly cheated out of the prize in a poetry competition.

They turned radical, too. The famous anarchist, Emma Goldman moved to the Village that year and began publishing a magazine she called *Mother Earth*. One of her neighbors was the dancer Isadora Duncan, who introduced the term "free love" to the language.

The Village had been previously discovered by Gertrude Vanderbilt Whitney, who bought a stable in Macdougal Alley behind the row of houses on Washington Square North to pursue a career as a sculptor. No matter that she was among the richest women in New York, she had other ideas and the peace and quiet of the Village was just perfect for developing them.

Others, like Eugene O'Neill and Edgar Allen Poe, had moved into rooms south of the Square where rents averaged about three dollars a week.

Added to the mix was the fashionable Brevoort Hotel, next door to Mrs. Dodge's Fifth Avenue house. It was the number one choice of European visitors, most of whom were considered more intellectual than the average American and many of whom were accomplished artists and writers. It wasn't long before Mrs. Dodge's stark white apartment became more popular with them than the Brevoort's cafe. After all, the company was better and the drinks and hors d'oeuvres were free.

People like Lincoln Steffens, Carl Van Vechten and Alfred Steiglitz shared the experience. It was Steffens who suggested that she expand her salon on a more organized basis. "It could revive the art of conversation," he told her. She began inviting people for "Evenings" once a week and before long discussions between Walter Lippman and Max Eastman, two Socialists with quite different points of view, or the views of birth control pioneer Margaret Sanger, expressed at Mrs. Dodge's Evenings, began appearing in the newspapers. Mrs. Dodge became famous and at the same time the Village began to have a reputation as a hotbed of radical thought. That was in spite of the fact that the discussions almost always gave equal time to traditional thought.

The activities at Mabel Dodge's salon were augmented by evenings at the Liberal Club, which met at Polly's Restaurant at 133 Macdougal Street. Conversations there regularly involved people like Theodore Dreiser and Sinclair Lewis or John Reed, a close associate of Mrs. Dodge, who Van Wyck Brooks called the "wonder boy of Greenwich Village." It eventually became the offices and living quarters of the staff of *The Masses* published by Max Eastman to get into print "what is too naked or true for the money-making press."

No wonder no one was surprised when, on New Year's Eve, 1916, a group of villagers including artists Marcel Duchamp and John Sloan climbed to the top of Washington Square Arch and, after firing cap pistols and releasing red balloons, declared the Village a "free republic, independent of Uptown." By "Uptown," they apparently meant the entire country because their Proclamation also included an appeal to President Wilson for Federal protection as a small country.

No one had seen anything yet. The Twenties were yet to roar.

The first two decades of Village Bohemianism were mostly intellectual. People got involved in social causes that ranged from education reform to birth control. They were passionate about righting the wrongs committed by the rest of society and altering the way the country had been going in its first 125 years. World War I began to change things in ways they hadn't anticipated. The 1917 Revolution in Russia produced a fear of Reds that almost bordered on national hysteria. It drove all but the most dedicated out of the ranks of Socialism. The intellectuals began moving from the Village into the suburbs. Even Mabel Dodge herself sold her Fifth Avenue house and moved to a farm in Westchester County. At the same time, as if to add insult to injury, the city extended the Seventh Avenue subway into the Village in 1917. It destroyed the neighborhood by barbarically widening the avenue to superhighway proportions. Worse, it made it easier for sightseers to get there. It was the last straw for many of the intellectuals who weren't amused when people stopped them on the street to ask "are you a Bohemian?".

But questions like that opened the door for a new breed of Village denizen, the sort who thrive on attention. One was a girl named Doris The Dope who made it a habit to cough as much as possible in the presence of tourists who she informed her problem was the result of posing nude for local artists. The poor thing was no dope at all. She made a lot of money that way. Another was one they called "The Baroness" who wore a peach basket for a hat and pasted postage stamps on her face as makeup. Yet another, who called himself "Tiny Tim," dispensed what he called "soul candy," which came wrapped in poetry he had written himself.

By 1919 it looked as though intellectualism was dead in Greenwich Village. But nobody seemed to care. They had other things to worry about. Drinking was about to become illegal.

During the '20s, the people who poured off the Seventh Avenue IRT weren't looking for Bohemians any longer. What they needed to find was a drink.

The Village was already established by them as a bastion of broad-mindedness and it was only natural that the easiest of the speak-easies should be located there. But in some places liquor was sold out in the open. One of them was the Greenwich Village Inn or Sheridan Square. When Prohibition became law, its owner, Barney Gallant, decided that he'd serve liquor, law or no law. He was arrested for his trouble and sentenced to thirty days in jail. It wasn't a popular decision. A petition circulated around the city and 20,000 people signed it, demanding Barney's release. By the time it got to the judge, the thirty days were up anyway and Barney was not only free but famous. And the fame of the Village as a wicked place spread a little bit further.

Of course you could get a drink in the Village during the Prohibition years. And the Village speak-easies were more likely to be small mom-and-pop affairs which were more pleasant and quaint if not quieter and less flashy than the uptown establishments in the mid-Fifties. The result was that the Village attracted a younger, more impressionable crowd. And the impression they got was that of a kind of free and easy tolerance.

In the years after the First World War, the last of the radical thinkers took their ideas to Europe and the image of Greenwich Village began to change again. But if it was different, it was only a matter of degree. Three people were responsible and they were all writers: Willa Cather, who moved to

Bank Street, Theodore Dreiser, who lived on Saint Luke's Place, and Sherwood Anderson, who lived next door to him. All three were well-established before moving there and their presence lured others like them, including the poet Edna St. Vincent Millay, who came to New York looking for a career as an actress.

By 1925, about half the important literature in the United States was written in Greenwich Village apartments. Artists abounded there, too, but it was the writers who lured young people from all parts of the country looking for a life of creativity in a picturesque atmosphere.

Their fame lured tourists, too, and new restaurants and jazz clubs were established to give them what they were looking for. It was a gay, carefree place where anyone could find almost anything they might be looking for, always with a deceptively quaint, charming touch. Young girls, fresh out of college and armed with monthly checks from their daddies, began renting apartments in the Village and walking the streets wearing colorful smocks that were, along with bobbed hair, a universal sign of liberation. Though they spent most of their time trying to make a typewriter produce a cohesive sentence, they worked hard at cultivating an air of possible wickedness that did more to attract young men than all the cohesive sentences ever written.

The excitement lasted right up until the fall of 1929 when events in Wall Street changed Manhattan in general and the Village in particular into something no one ever dreamed could happen.

The Great Depression stopped the flow of money that had kept the whole thing going. Artists and writers lost their patrons. The parents of would-be writers stopped sending checks. Sightseers couldn't afford the restaurants and jazz clubs that had been established for their pleasure. "Creativity" became less important than figuring out where the next dollar might come from. Though the Bohemian life had always been Spartan, now that the whole country shared that experience there was no special reason to go to Greenwich Village.

When World War II came along, the Village became a "must see" attraction for GIs passing through, and newer attractions were added to cater to them. But the things people had come to see during the previous forty years had gone elsewhere. Eugene O'Neill had moved to California, Edna St. Vincent Millay moved back to New England.

When the war was over, rents began going up — they haven't stopped climbing yet — and a new kind of Villager began moving in. Today's resident is more likely to be a highly-paid advertising executive or soap opera star. Yet today's atmosphere is almost no different than it was forty years ago, and visitors are almost never disappointed. The surroundings are the same, and so is the attitude. On an island where change is part of the excitement, this section of it thrives on lack of change. Oddly, though no one ever intended it that way, Greenwich Village is an anchor of stability in a place that never seems quite satisfied with the way it is.

Times Square is as important as any section of Manhattan as a place every visitor has to see before calling a trip to New York complete. Yet almost no one is pleased with the way it is. Over the last dozen years, all sorts of interested groups have announced that they have the perfect plan to "clean up Times Square." The most acceptable one so far seems to please the folks who make money tearing down "obsolete" buildings and replacing them with massive towers. Whether it will actually happen or not in Times Square is still open to question, but Broadway types, who will bet on anything, aren't taking any bets that Times Square won't change dramatically into a relatively sterile office district within our lifetime.

But Times Square, like all the rest of Manhattan, has seen dramatic change before.

It wasn't even called Times Square until *The New York Times* built a tower in the triangle between Broadway and Seventh Avenue at 42d Street in 1904. Until then it was known as Longacre Square and it was well-known as the place to buy a horse or a new carriage. The same year *The Times* moved uptown from the City Hall area, the first subway line was opened from City Hall to Grand Central Terminal and then west to Broadway where it turned north again to run uptown under Broadway. Times Square became one of its major stops and eventually one of the main intersections of the new lines that were added.

The Metropolitan Opera House had been operating two blocks south on Broadway for more than 20 years by then and entrepreneurs like Oscar Hammerstein were operating theaters to the north of the new Times Tower. By the end of the 1920s there were more than 70 theaters flourishing in the area and they were surrounded by elegant hotels and fine restaurants created to serve their patrons.

Forty-Second Street between Seventh and Eighth Avenues was at the heart of it all with the best theaters, the best restaurants. Today it's a block of less-than-attractive movie theaters and a street population like something out of a bad movie.

In 1891, an advertising genius put a huge electric sign at the corner of 23d Street and Broadway to lure homebuyers to Brooklyn's Manhattan Beach. A PR genius declared that it made Broadway "the Great White Way" and it was inevitable that more such signs would follow. The next leap was to the 34th Street area where many of the signs became tourist attractions. But it all developed into a fine art in the late 1930s when an Englishman named Douglas Leigh began calling them "spectaculars" and began placing them in the Times Square area. He constructed one for the Bond Clothing store in a converted theater between 44th and 45th Street that included a waterfall almost a block wide flanked by two sculptured nudes that were almost as tall as the building itself. When Pepsi Cola bought the space, the nudes were replaced with soft drink bottles, but the waterfall remained.

Leigh was also responsible for hiding the front of the Claridge Hotel on Broadway between 43d and 44th Streets, behind a sign for Camel Cigarettes that featured the face of a contented smoker blowing smoke rings down on the crowd below.

Across the street, the crowds were lined up to see the movie and the stage show at the Paramount Theater. A block north of there, across from the waterfall, they were meeting friends at the Astor Hotel. Both landmarks have long-since been replaced by office space, as has the Claridge Hotel where the smoker held forth.

The planners say that the "new" Times Square will also have electric signs and other bright lights. Change has come to that aspect of the Square already. There are no "spectaculars" of the sort Douglas Leigh dreamed up — he has found a new career designing the lighting for the tops of Manhattan's skyscrapers. The job of producing electric advertising signs seems to have been taken over by Japanese companies to promote electronic and photographic gadgets. In spite of all their technological prowess, the element of imagination is missing and they seem overly impressed by the design effects produced by the shape of the letters in the Western alphabet, just as we are with theirs.

Be that as it may, while they've changed the face of Times Square, at least they've kept the lights burning. A clue to why more American advertising agencies don't recommend Times Square electric signs to their clients came in the late 1970s when the moving sign that once flashed news bulletins around the Times Tower went dark. The real estate speculator who owned the building at the time announced that he was letting it happen because the people who hang out in Times Square weren't worth the effort. (Probable English translation: its operation cut into profits.)

For all that happens to change the appearance of this island called Manhattan, a thing that doesn't change appreciably is the attitude of the people. Manhattanites don't wear "I Love New York" buttons lightly. They're fiercely proud of the place and the fact that they're part of it. If there are things they don't like, they know it will probably change and possibly change for the better. And they know that if they want to they can have a say in what sort of change takes place. It's been called the biggest small town in America and it probably is. More accurately, it's the biggest *collection* of small towns in America, and that may be the secret of success. Instead of trying to influence change on the whole island, the average Manhattanite does it in small bites in individual neighborhoods. And, yes, they do know their neighbors. They care about them, too. After all, it isn't possible to live in the midst of so many other people and not notice them. Besides, so many of them are so interesting. And that, more than anything else, is what makes Manhattan so fascinating!

Liberty Enlightening the World, *better known as the Statue of Liberty (previous page and facing page top), was presented to the United States on July 4, 1886, by France at the suggestion of its sculptor, Frédéric Auguste Bartholdi. She was raised, with the aid of framework built by Alexandre Gustave Eiffel, at the entrance to New York Harbor (facing page bottom). Above: the 1931 Empire State Building. At night the top thirty floors are lit up in colors that alter with the occasion. Overleaf: the World Trade Center behind Cesar Pelli's copper-domed World Financial Center buildings.*

Midtown Manhattan (these pages and overleaf) is dominated by the tower (facing page) bearing the name given to New York: "the Empire State." With 102 stories, it was the world's tallest structure from the time of its completion in May 1931 until 1954. The Art Deco Chrysler Building (above), with its elegant spire, was constructed in 1930 by William Van Alen for Walter P. Chrysler, the automobile manufacturer. The building is decorated with friezes and gargoyles made up of representations of car parts! When built, it was the first structure to surpass France's Eiffel Tower in height.

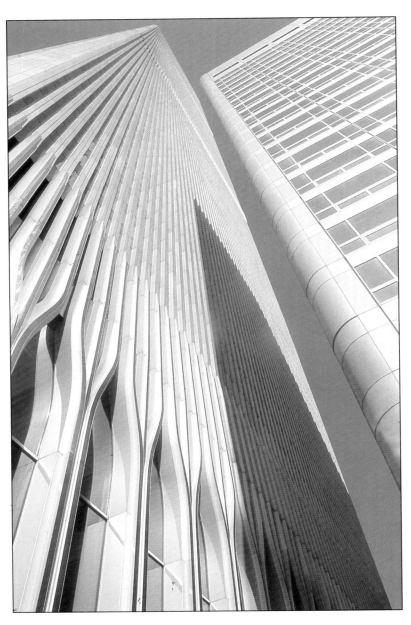

New Yorkers have been noted for their ingenuity ever since July 9, 1776, when discontented locals toppled the statue of George III in Bowling Green and melted it down for bullets to use against his Redcoats. Faced later with the problem of limited land and unlimited aspirations, New York looked up. The first office elevator appeared here in 1871 and, with the development of steel construction, the skyscraper was born. With the push of Manhattan's buildings ever upwards, some city streets became like shady canyon floors, with the lines of the buildings drawing the eye skyward. From the observation deck of the World Trade Center (facing page top left and bottom) one can have a spectacular view of New York and beyond. Above: the World Financial Center and Twin Towers, and (overleaf) Uptown by night, its streets like rivers of molten light.

34

These pages and overleaf: Fifth Avenue. This is one of New York's most famous thoroughfares,
dividing Manhattan into east and west as it runs centrally through the city, alongside Central Park
for some of the way, between Washington Square and the Harlem River. Some of Manhattan's finest
retail centers are found on Fifth Avenue, among them Saks and Tiffany's.

Above: Bryant Park, and (facing page) the Plaza Hotel, overlooking Central Park (top and overleaf).
Built in a French Renaissance-style with a mansard roof, the hotel is the work of Henry J.
Hardenbergh. The Times *enthusiastically wrote of the opening of the Plaza: "the design is so*
successful that the building looms up a welcome addition to the skyline of middle Manhattan."

These pages: Fulton Landing, and (overleaf) Pier 17, both part of South Street Seaport on the East River. Fulton Landing is named for Robert Fulton, who designed the first successful steamboat after quitting an unpromising career as an artist. South Street Seaport is the last vestige of a nineteenth-century port in Manhattan and several sailing ships are moored here at restored piers overlooked by the old, Federal-style brick houses of Schermerhorn Row. At Pier 15 a visiting ship is moored across from the resident German bark Peking, built in 1911, her four yellow masts standing up against the modern skyline. Peking, built in Hamburg, was originally used to ship guano from Chile to Europe.

The New York Stock Exchange (this page and overleaf) was founded beneath a buttonwood tree on May 17, 1792. Only the sculpture of a tree at the entrance to the building hints at such humble beginnings. Today the Stock Exchange is housed in a Grecian-style "temple" built in 1903 to the designs of George G. Post. There is nothing classical about the trading floor (overleaf), however, where modern machines deal in wealth. Outside, facing Broad Street, the 1833 statue of George Washington by J.Q.A. Ward stands before Federal Hall (facing page). Washington took his presidential oath in 1789 from the balcony of the original building.

These pages: the business architecture of Midtown Manhattan (overleaf). Above: the Grand Hyatt Hotel. Facing page: (top right) the IBM Building Plaza, and (bottom left) the Trump Tower. Donald Trump described skyscrapers as a "combination of ego and a desire for financial gain."

The United Nations Headquarters (left) stands on the banks of the East River upon eighteen acres of land donated by John D. Rockefeller, Jr. Prior to its redevelopment this land, known then as Turtle Bay, was covered in slums, breweries and slaughter houses. Today, technically, this area is not part of America, but a state within a state. Overleaf: Pier 17 of South Street Seaport Museum, also on the East River.

Times Square (right), like other Manhattan
"squares" is not actually a square at all, but an
intersection – in this case of Broadway and
Seventh Avenue. Until 1904 it was known as
Longacre Square, but the name was changed when
the New York Times occupied the premises at
Number One. The paper has since moved around
the corner, but the name Times Square stuck and
trucks emblazoned with "New York Times" are
still a frequent sight. Overleaf: the skyline around
the Empire State Building at night.

Above: the Winter Garden, also known as Crystal Palace, part of the World Financial Center Complex in Battery Park City (overleaf), behind which loom the twin towers of the World Trade Center. Architect of the World Financial Center, Cesar Pelli, said of his buildings: "They hold their own ... I have absorbed the World Trade Center towers beyond and made them gentler." In the evening sun, glinting gold and bronze, they look as opulent as if they were wearing the wealth they create. Facing page: (bottom) Queensboro Bridge, and (top) 1883 Brooklyn Bridge. The latter was the first to span the East River, built by engineer John A. Roebling and his son Washington to make Manhattan more easily accessible by linking downtown Manhattan with downtown Brooklyn. Queensboro Bridge was built in 1909 by Henry Hornbostel to connect Queens with Manhattan.

These pages: St. Patrick's Cathedral, Fifth Avenue. James Renwick designed this Roman Catholic cathedral, seat of the Archbishop of New York, after the Gothic cathedrals of Amiens and Cologne. It took years to complete; work began in 1858 and finished in 1906. At the time of completion parishioners complained that it was too far out of town! The subsequent, speedy northward expansion of Manhattan has since corrected that. This huge church seats up to 2,500 people and its organ has more than 9,000 pipes. It was dedicated to St. Patrick in 1910.

Facing page top: Washington Arch, the work of architect Stanford White, "gateway" to Greenwich Village at the end of Fifth Avenue in Washington Square Park. Facing page bottom: the Lower Plaza of Rockefeller Center, dominated by Paul Manship's 1934, gold-leafed statue Prometheus. Top: one of the many shady avenues of Central Park. Above: Grove Court, a select residential part of Greenwich Village. Built in the 1850s for "workingmen," it is now home to famous writers and artists.

"Prometheus, teacher in every art, brought the fire that hath proved to mortals a means to mighty ends." So reads the inscription behind Paul Manship's golden statue Prometheus (top) in Rockefeller Center's Lower Plaza. Above: the McGraw-Hill Plaza. Facing page: (top) the Metropolitan Opera House, known more familiarly as the "Met," in the Lincoln Center for the Performing Arts, and (bottom) the atrium of the 1977 Citicorp Center on Lexington Avenue in Midtown Manhattan.

Facing page: the Plaza Hotel, built in 1907, opposite the sunken General Motors Plaza and mirrored to one side by 9 West 57th Street, a fifty-story office building. The golden statue of General Tecumseh Sherman (above) by Augustus Saint-Gaudens overlooks the Plaza and 9 West 57th Street from Grand Army Plaza on Fifth Avenue. Overleaf: Midtown Manhattan and the Hudson.

Right: Midtown Manhattan with the Chrysler Building in the center. When Walter Chrysler commissioned his building in the late '20s, he envisaged putting his name to the tallest building in the world. However, a few months before his edifice was completed, the Manhattan Company thwarted him with their 927-foot-tall Wall Street tower. Chrysler, who didn't admit defeat that easily, instructed his architect, William Van Alen, to create a stainless steel spire to supplement his design. It was secretly smuggled into the unfinished building and raised up through the roof, giving the Chrysler Building sixty feet on the Manhattan Company! But Chrysler's glory was short-lived for in 1931 the Empire State Building took the crown. Whether motivated by pique or not, Chrysler refused an invitation to the grand opening of the Empire State, pleading a prior engagement. Overleaf: Manhattan from Weehawken, New Jersey.

Facing page: the Trump Tower, sixty-eight stories of office accommodation built on Fifth Avenue and 57th Street by the real estate developer, Donald John Trump, who modestly styles it: "the world's most talked about address." The logistics of building such a structure in Manhattan are formidable. To construct Trump Tower, nearly 90,000 tons of concrete, 3,800 tons of steel rods and 5,000 workers had to be transported there through streets locked with traffic. Such statistics notwithstanding, Trump Tower was completed in just three years. Above and overleaf: the covered plaza of the IBM Building on East 57th Street.

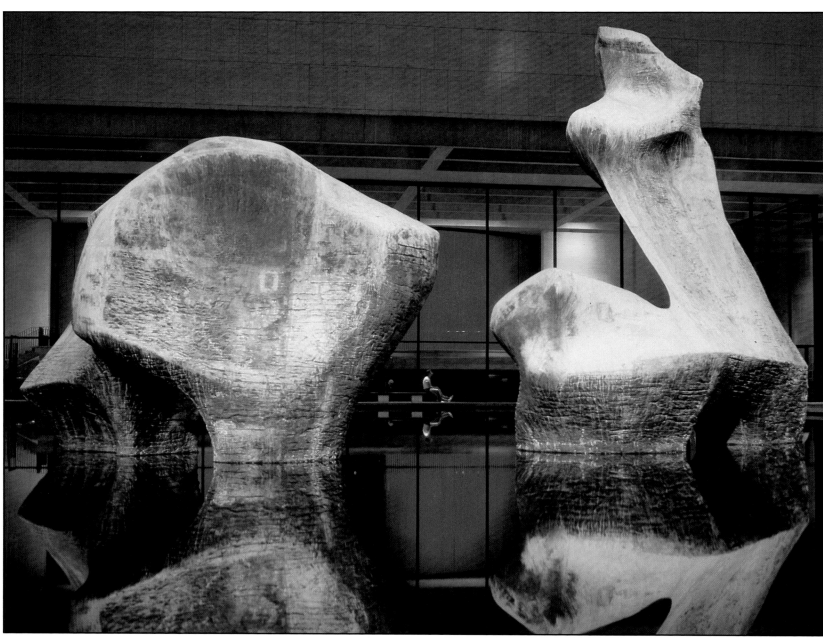

Facing page: the Solomon R. Guggenheim Museum on Fifth Avenue at 89th Street. Guggenheim, a copper magnate, was a collector of modern painting and established a foundation for the promotion and teaching of "non-objective art." In 1943 he earmarked $2 million for a museum which he commissioned Frank Lloyd Wright to build, but he died seven years before construction began in 1956. The museum was completed in 1959, and is one of Wright's most controversial structures. Its shape has been likened scathingly to many things: a mushroom, a corkscrew, a UFO; but Wright defiantly stated that one should no more judge a building by its exterior alone than a car by its color. Above: Henry Moore's Recling Figure in the Lincoln Center, and (top) Sphere for Plaza Fountain by Fritz Koenig standing in Austin J. Tobin Plaza between the towers of the World Trade Center.

The idea of Liberty (right) was born of an after-dinner discussion in 1865 among French thinkers who still espoused some of the principles of the French Revolution: liberty, equality and fraternity. It was the host, Edouard René Lefebvre de Laboulaye, who proposed a present to the American nation of a monument to American Independence for their 1876 Centennial, and guest, Bartholdi, who began to work on the design. He visited the States in 1871 to choose a site upon which to erect his masterpiece, and when he saw Bedloe's Island in New York Harbor said: "Here … my statue must rise; here where people get their first view of the New World." Overleaf: Pier 17 of South Street Seaport, seen from Brooklyn.

Facing page top: (left) the Municipal Building, and (right) D.H. Burnham's 1902 Flatiron Building, built to fit the junction of Fifth Avenue and 23rd Street. Facing page bottom: (left) St. Patrick's Cathedral, next door to Saks, and (right) Lee Lawrie's bronze Atlas Bearing the Heavens, outside the International Building in Rockefeller Center. On its installation, Lawrie's statue was picketed for its alleged resemblance to Mussolini. Above: Trump Tower, and (above right) the Chrysler Building. Top: the Empire State Building. Overleaf: Midtown Manhattan.

Fifth Avenue began, around 1824, as a socially sought-after residential area where the wealthy built opulent houses. By 1850, it was more fashionable than Broadway and home to the rich and famous, among the more illustrious being the Astors and Vanderbilts. These days it is still a fashionable residential area, but is perhaps even more famous for its shops and architecture.

These pages: Chinatown. The first Chinese to settle in New York were Cantonese sailors from the junk Kee Ying in 1847. About twenty years later their numbers were added to substantially by "coolies" who had been working on the transcontinental railway. Rivalries developed between immigrants from all over China with their different dialects and expectations. So many rival Chinese "tongs," or gangs, used to fight it out at the corner of Doyers and Pell streets that it was known as "bloody corner." It is considerably less volatile now, being more famous for its restaurants than its rivalries, and these days the tongs are respectable merchant associations.

Above: a view under Brooklyn Bridge toward Manhattan Bridge. Top: Broadway, and (facing page top) the Empire State Building lit up over the streets of SoHo (facing page bottom). SoHo, an acronym for South of Houston Street, is a favorite area among artists and musicians. It is also known for its cast-iron commercial architecture. The area used to be one of abandoned factories, warehouses and factory lofts, but artists saw great possibilities in these buildings for inexpensive studios, and SoHo's subsequent rise from deserted manufacturing base to fashionable artists' colony was rapid.

Facing page: the Empire State Building. The distinctive, gold-capped, illuminated pyramid (top) belongs to the Metropolitan Life Tower. Many of Manhattan's buildings rose in a fever of competitive construction. Height was the thing. For example, when Frank W. Woolworth put up his tower in 1914 he instructed his architect to make it bigger than the Metropolitan Life Tower, then the tallest, because Metropolitan Life Insurance had once refused him a loan! Above: Brooklyn Bridge and, beyond it, Manhattan Bridge spanning the East River from Manhattan to Brooklyn. Overleaf: dusk over Manhattan.

Left and overleaf: Orchard Street, Lower East Side. Orchard Street is closed to traffic on Sundays, allowing bargain-hunters to throng the streets and check out the many clothing stores.

Novelist James Fenimore Cooper wrote: "New York is essentially national in interest, position, pursuits. No one thinks of the place as belonging to a particular state, but to the United States." But with New York's ethnic diversity, it could also be described as international. Facing page: (top) Anthony Dapolito, proud proprietor of the Vesuvio Bakery in Little Italy, and (bottom) Orchard Street, in Jewish Lower East Side. Little Italy (this page) is full of fast food places selling Italian bread and pasta, German pretzels, Jewish bagels, and all-American burgers. Overleaf: Midtown Manhattan.

Left: Brooklyn Bridge, and (overleaf) Manhattan Bridge. Brooklyn Bridge was the first bridge to link Manhattan and Brooklyn, and is the second oldest in New York, after High Bridge on the Harlem River. Its construction was a mammoth and dangerous undertaking. German-born engineer John Augustus Roebling, the man who dared to build the suspended Railroad Bridge over Niagara Falls, began work in 1869. However, while on site his foot was crushed in an accident, gangrene set in and he died three weeks after an operation to amputate. His son, Washington, then took over, but another construction accident meant that he had to oversee the bridge's completion from his sickbed. The bridge was finally finished in 1883, having cost $25,000,000. Manhattan Bridge, the next to span the East River, was completed in 1909.

*These pages: Central Park in the fall. Its 843 acres constituting the largest open space in Manhattan,
Central Park was the idea of poet William Cullen Bryant, who, in 1844, suggested buying the land
and setting it aside for common recreation. In 1858, Frederick Law Olmsted and his partner Calvert
Vaux submitted their Greensward Plan for the landscaping of Central Park, which Olmsted
envisioned as "a democratic development of the highest significance," a park open to everyone.
Overleaf: the tulips and cherry trees of Battery Park.*

At dusk Manhattan looks deceptively tranquil, but the lights of Times Square (overleaf) illuminate Manhattan's busy nightlife. Above: Pier 3, Brooklyn docks, and (top) New York Harbor. Under a heavy sinking sun Liberty (facing page) raises her torch from Bedloe's Island. Emma Lazarus saw her not so much as a classical figure than as the "Mother of Exiles" when she wrote the famous lines that appear on Liberty's pedestal: "Give me your tired, your poor, your huddled masses yearning to breathe free..." that inspired past newcomers to America on their way to another famous New York Harbor destination, Ellis Island.

Right: Brooklyn Bridge at night, hung with lights. Overleaf: the World Financial Center, Battery Park City, with the dome of the Winter Garden, or Crystal Palace, lit up like a bulb. Following page: Liberty in the silver waters of New York Harbor.

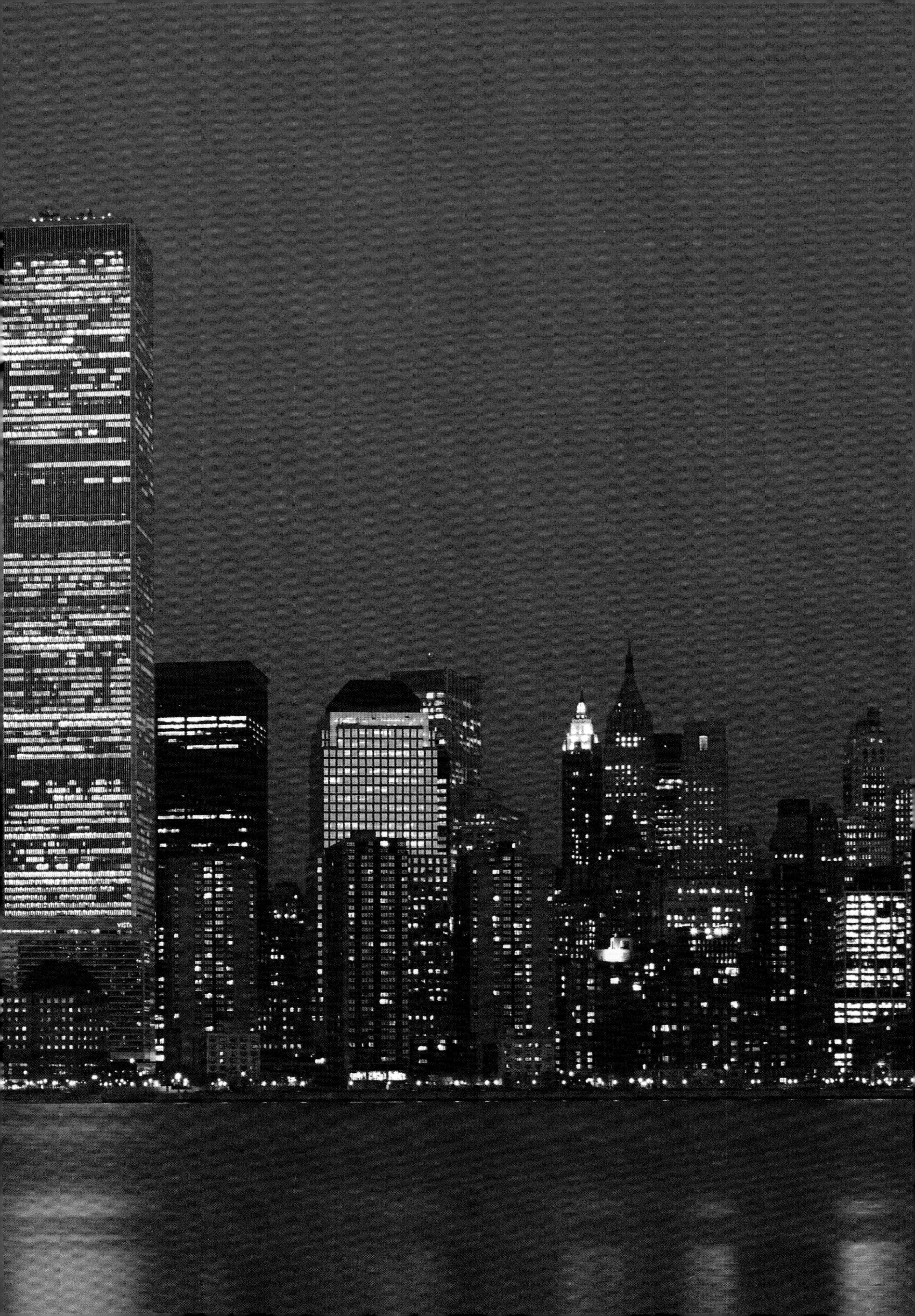

INDEX

9 West 57th Street 72
Austin J. Tobin Plaza 84
Battery Park 118, 119
Battery Park City 24, 25, 31, 64, 65, 126, 127
Broadway 98
Brooklyn Bridge 63, 98, 101, 112, 113, 124, 125
Brooklyn Docks 120
Bryant Park 38
Central Park 38, 40, 41, 69, 116, 117
Chinatown 96, 97
   Doyer Street 96
Chrysler Building 26, 52, 53, 76, 77, 91, 92, 93
Citicorp Center 71
Empire State Building 22, 27, 52, 53, 60, 61, 74, 75, 91, 99,
   100
Federal Hall 47
Fifth Avenue 34, 35, 36, 37, 94, 95
Flatiron Building 90
General Tecumseh Sherman Statue 73
George Washington Statue 47
Grand Army Plaza 73
Grand Hyatt Hotel 50
Grove Court 69
Guggenheim Museum 85
Hotel Pierre 73
IBM Building 51, 80, 82, 83
Liberty, Statue of 21, 23, 86, 87, 121, 128
Lincoln Center 71

Metropolitan Opera House 71
   Reclining Figure Statue 84
Little Italy 108, 109
Manhattan Bridge 98, 101, 114, 115
McGraw-Hill Plaza 70
Metropolitan Life Building 101
Municipal Building 90
New York Harbor 23, 120
New York Stock Exchange 46, 48, 49
Orchard Street 104, 105, 106, 107, 109
Plaza Hotel 39, 72
Queensboro Bridge 63
Rockefeller Center 68, 70
   Atlas Bearing the Heavens Statue 90
   International Building 90
   Lower Plaza 68, 70
   Prometheus Statue 68, 70
SoHo 99
South Street Seaport 42-45, 56, 57, 88, 89
   Fulton Landing 42, 43
   Pier 17 44, 45, 56, 57, 88, 89
St. Patrick's Cathedral 66, 67, 90
Times Square 58, 59, 122, 123
Trump Tower 51, 80, 91
United Nations Headquarters 54, 55
Washington Arch 68
World Financial Center 24, 25, 31, 62, 64, 65, 126, 127
World Trade Center 24, 25, 30, 31, 64, 65, 126, 127